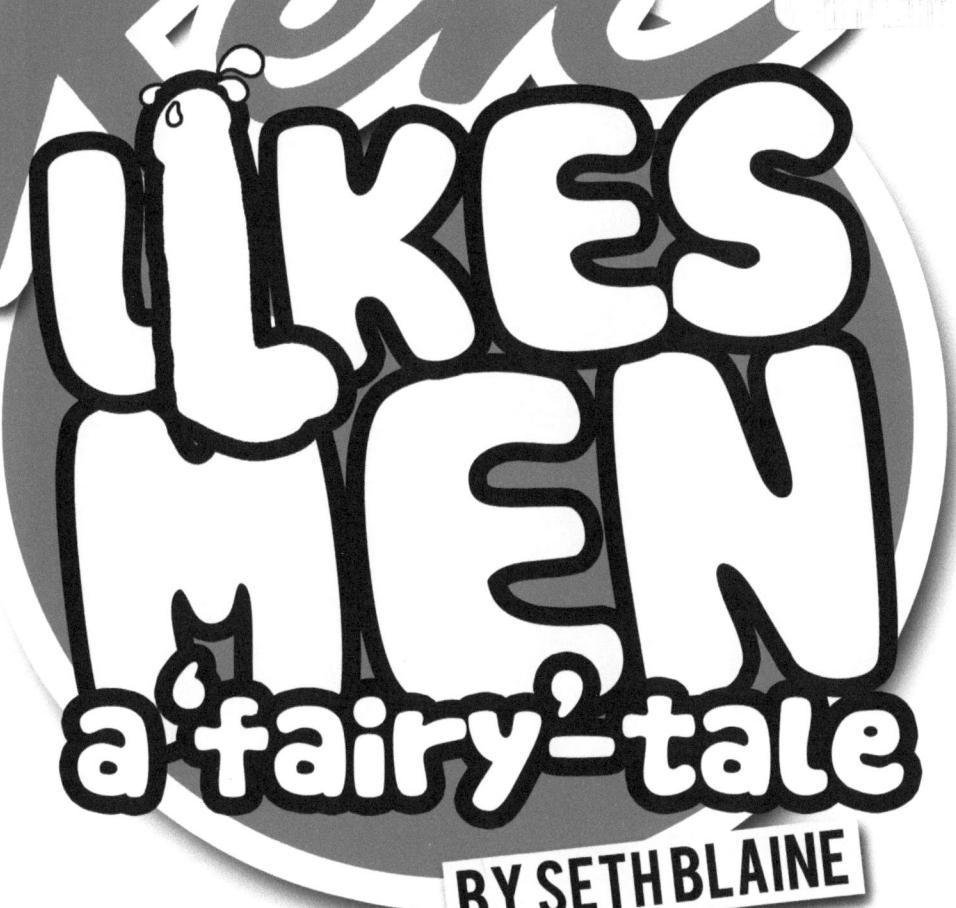

Ken LIKES MEN
a 'fairy' tale

BY SETH BLAINE

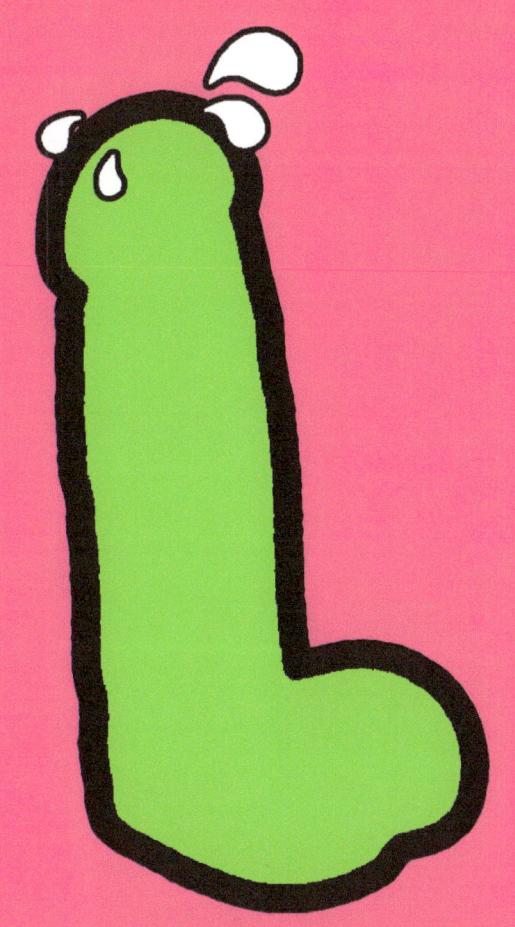

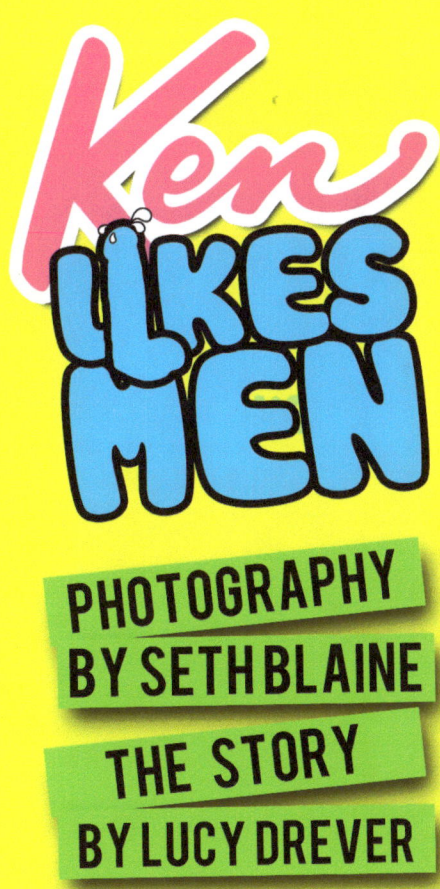

Ken
LIKES MEN

PHOTOGRAPHY
BY SETH BLAINE

THE STORY
BY LUCY DREVER

If of a nervous disposition, look away now! NO SERIOUSLY. ITS SICK.

Once upon a time in a land far away,
lived Barbie and Ken,
but Ken was gay.

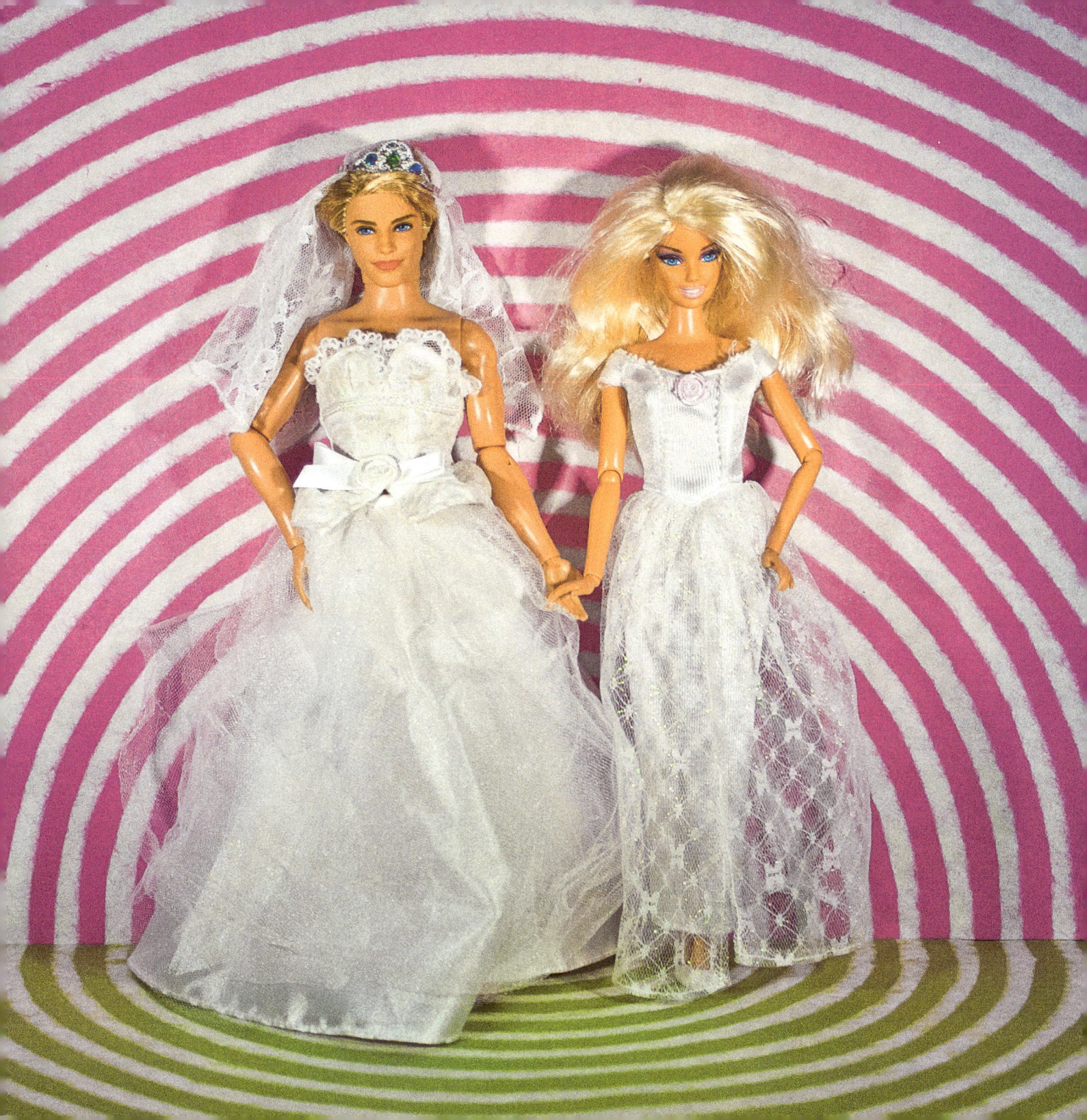

Barbie had her suspicions, which were growing. Ken had some hobbies, which had begun showing.

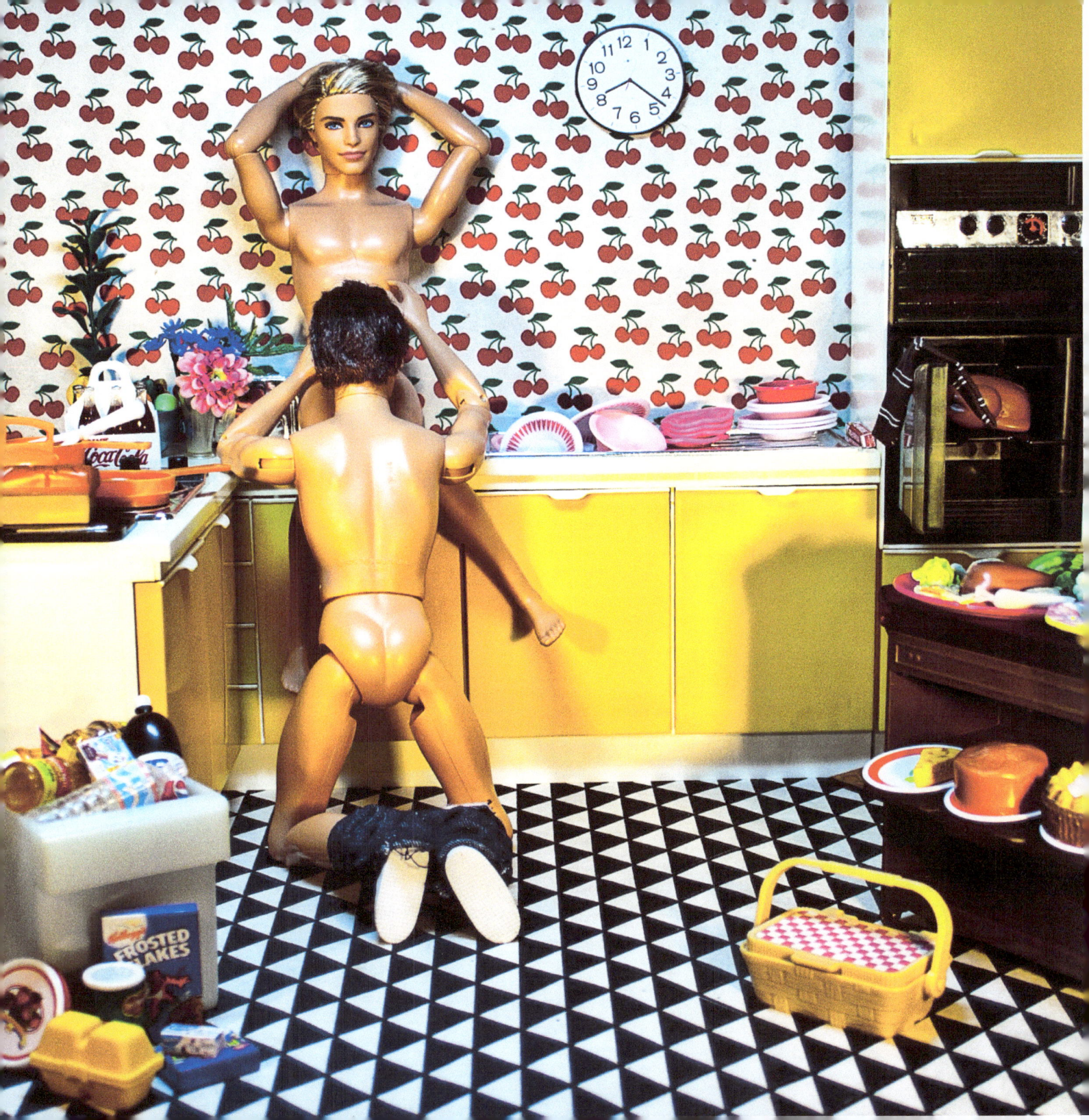

A porn magazine found in her
bed, Oh so peculiar she
scratched her head.

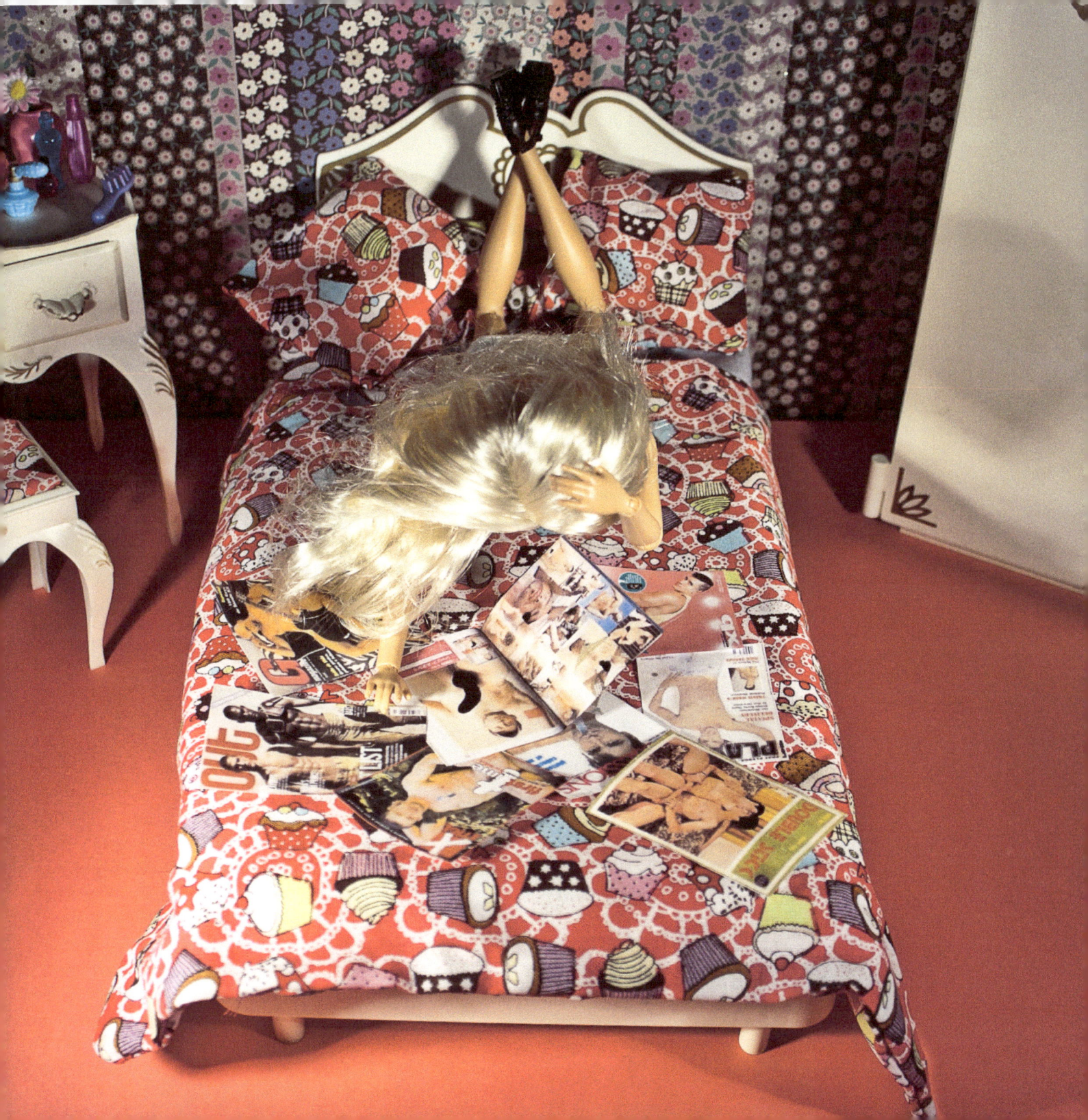

Barbie s old clothes suddenly dirty, though she hadn t worn them since she was thirty.

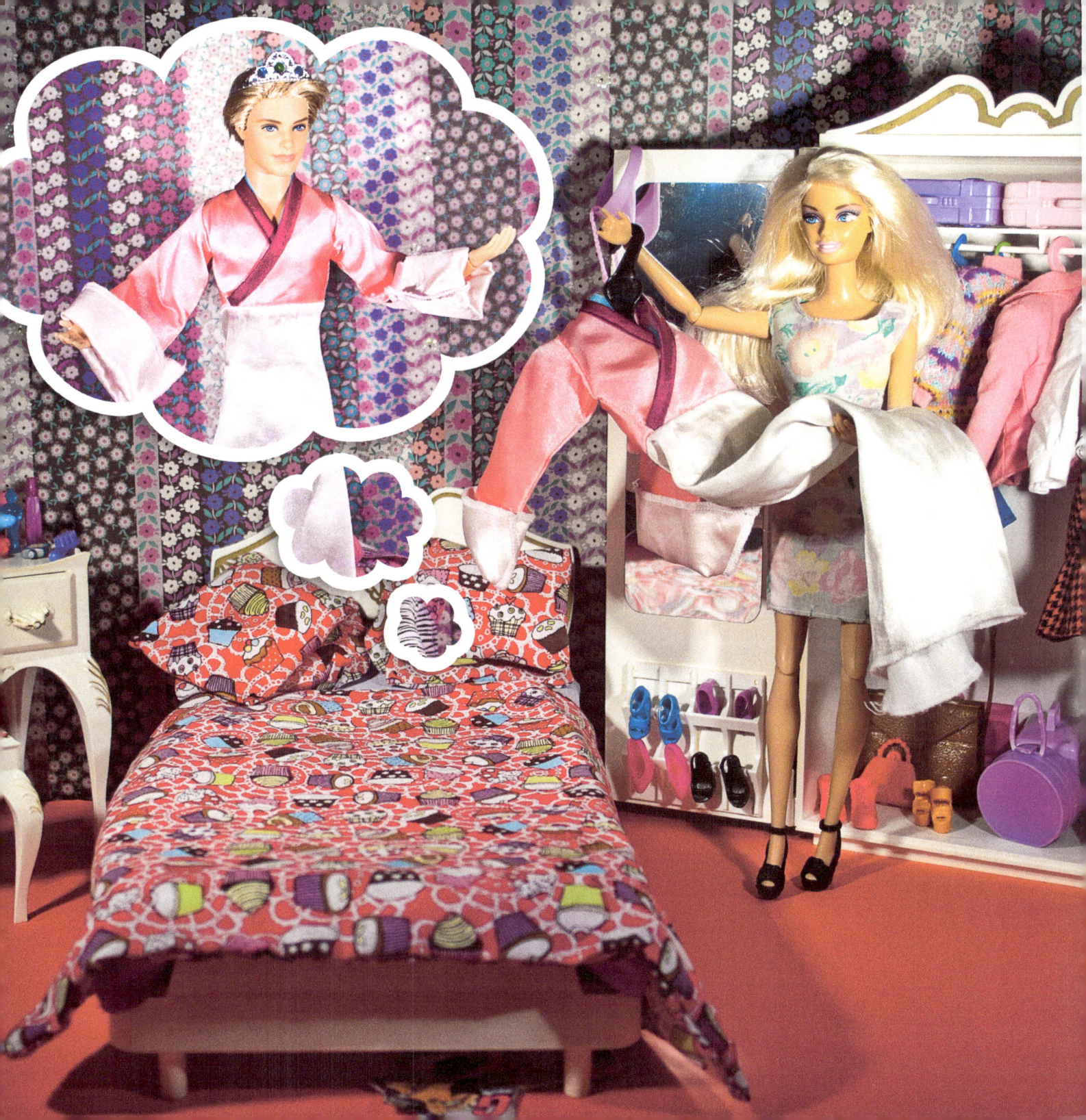

Barbie ignored this and got on with
her life, the lies were spreading,
the rumours were rife.

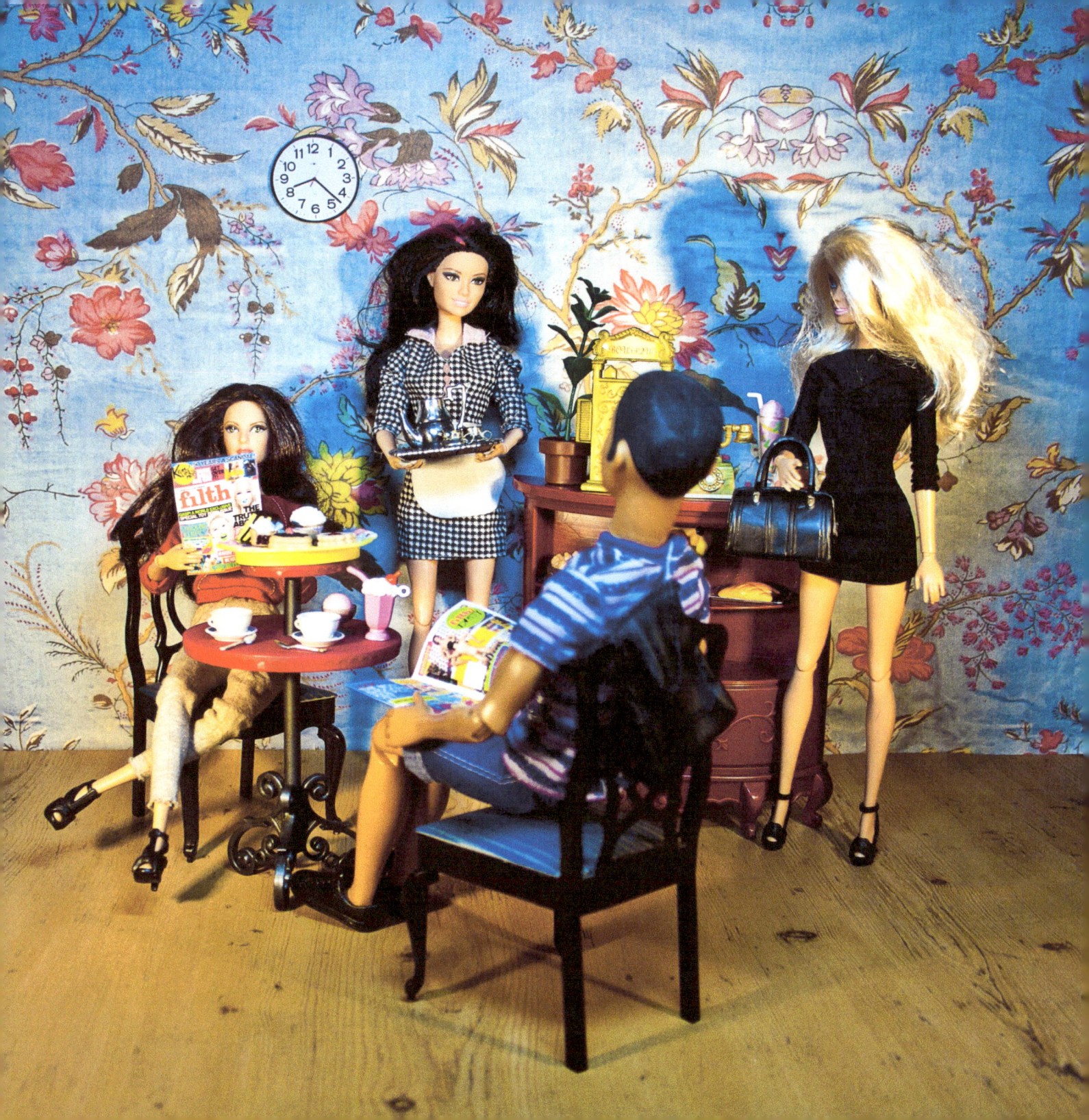

SHE KNEW THAT KEN WAS HIDING A
SECRET, KEN WASN T SURE HOW LONG HE
COULD KEEP IT.

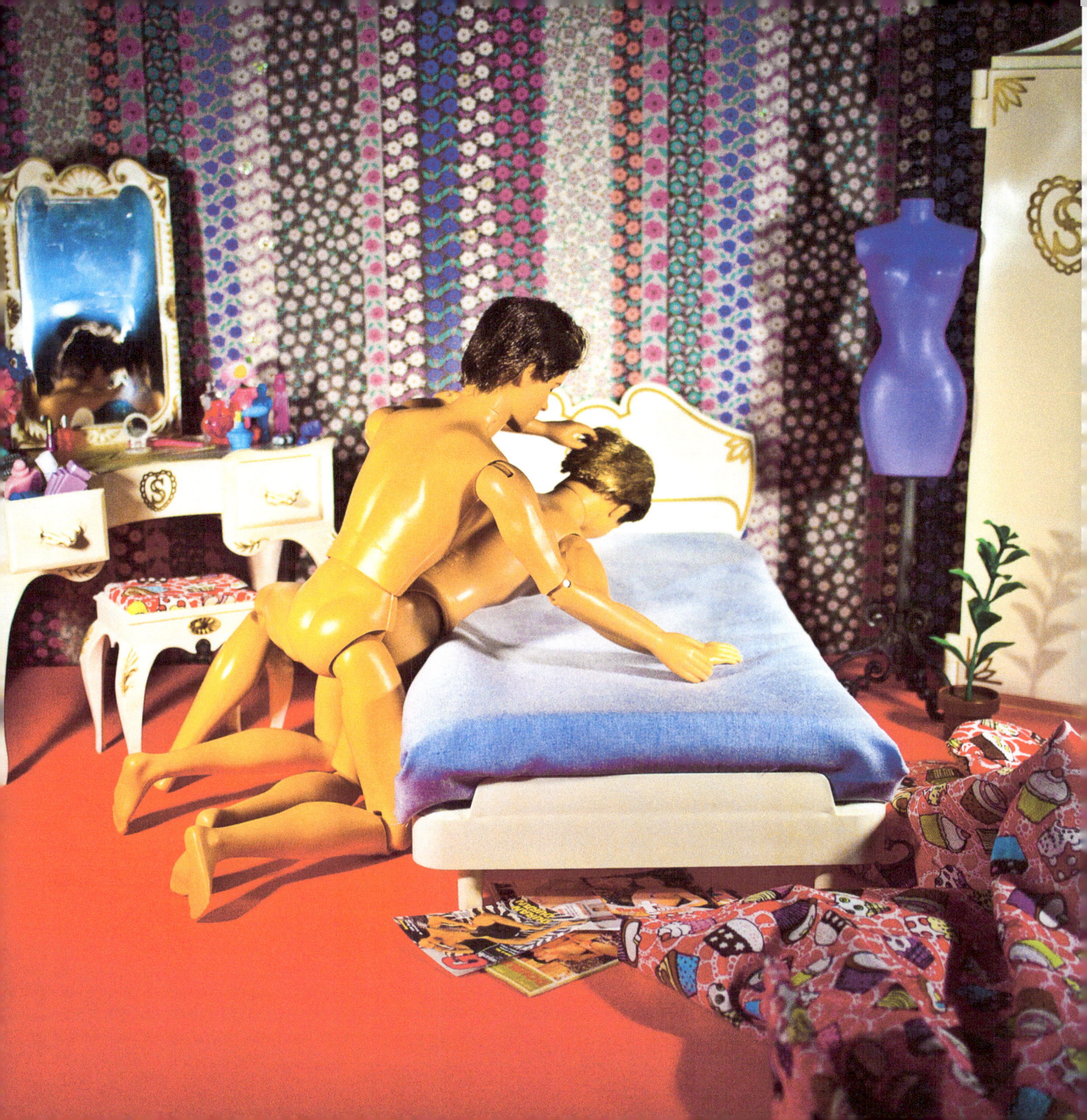

Printed there, as the latest scandal, a picture had leaked of Ken fisting Randall!

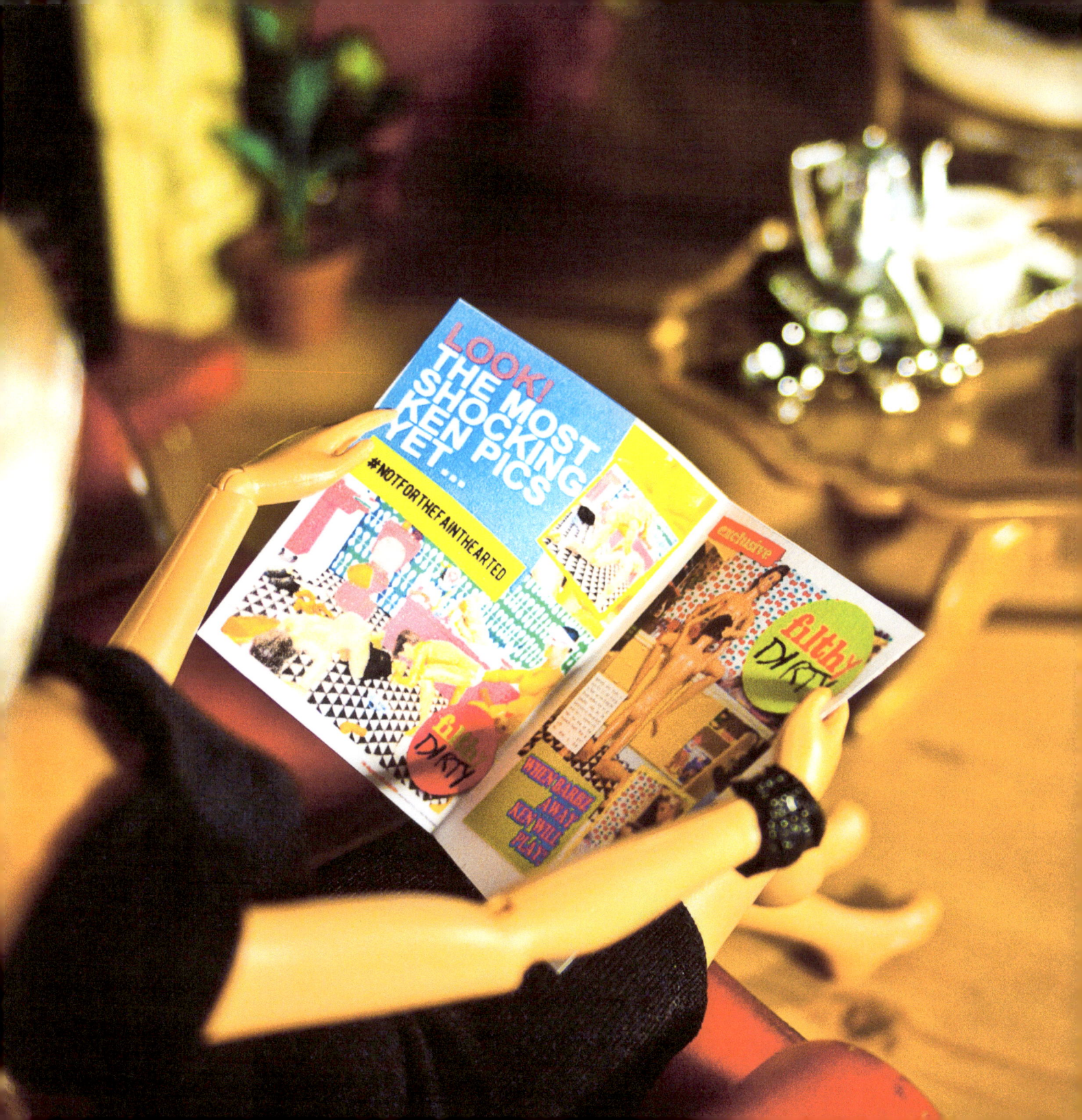

Reading the stories in her favourite mag, Barbie was shocked...her husband was a fag!

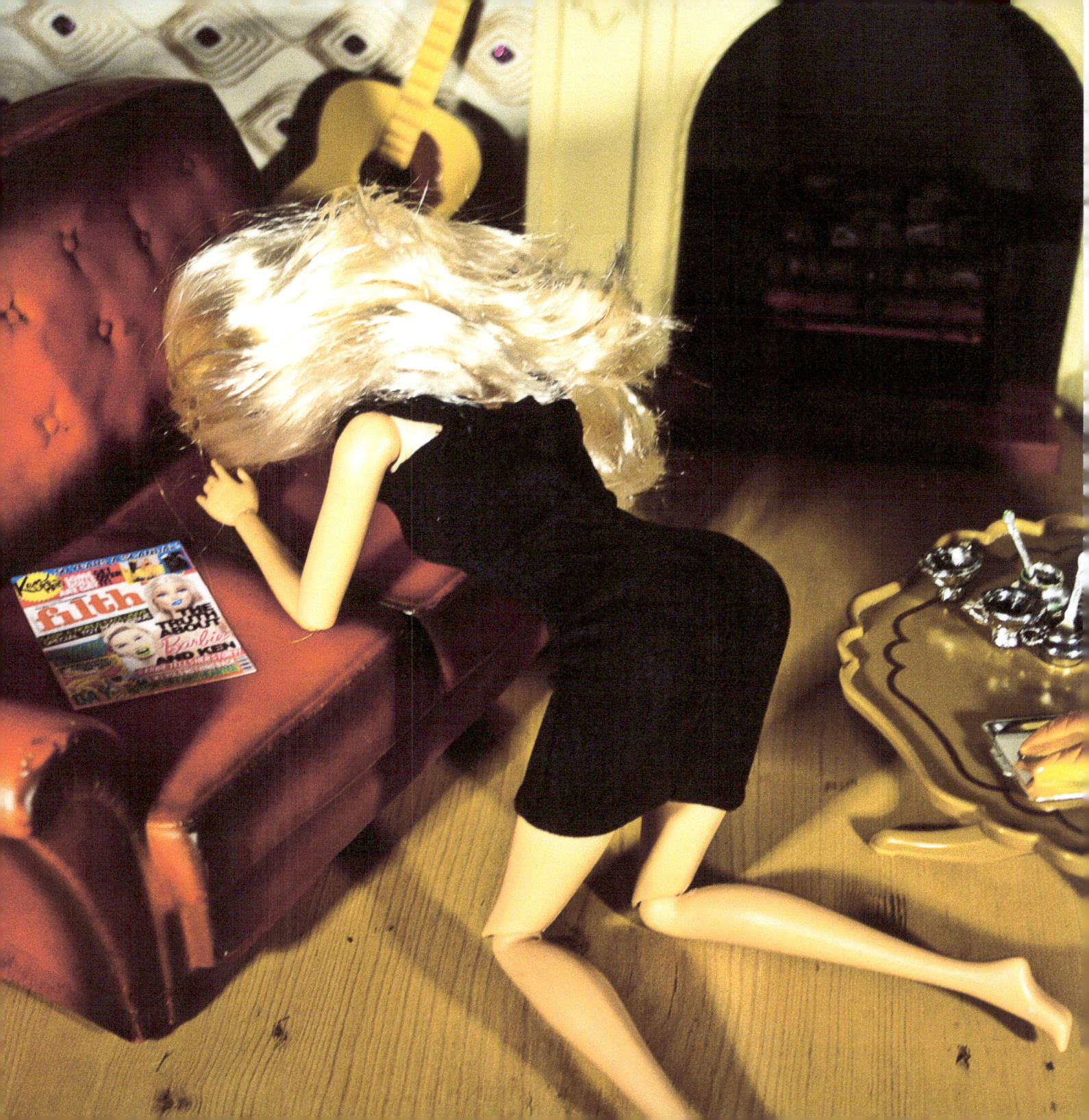

Ken was out having a drink; Barbie
was home she started to think.

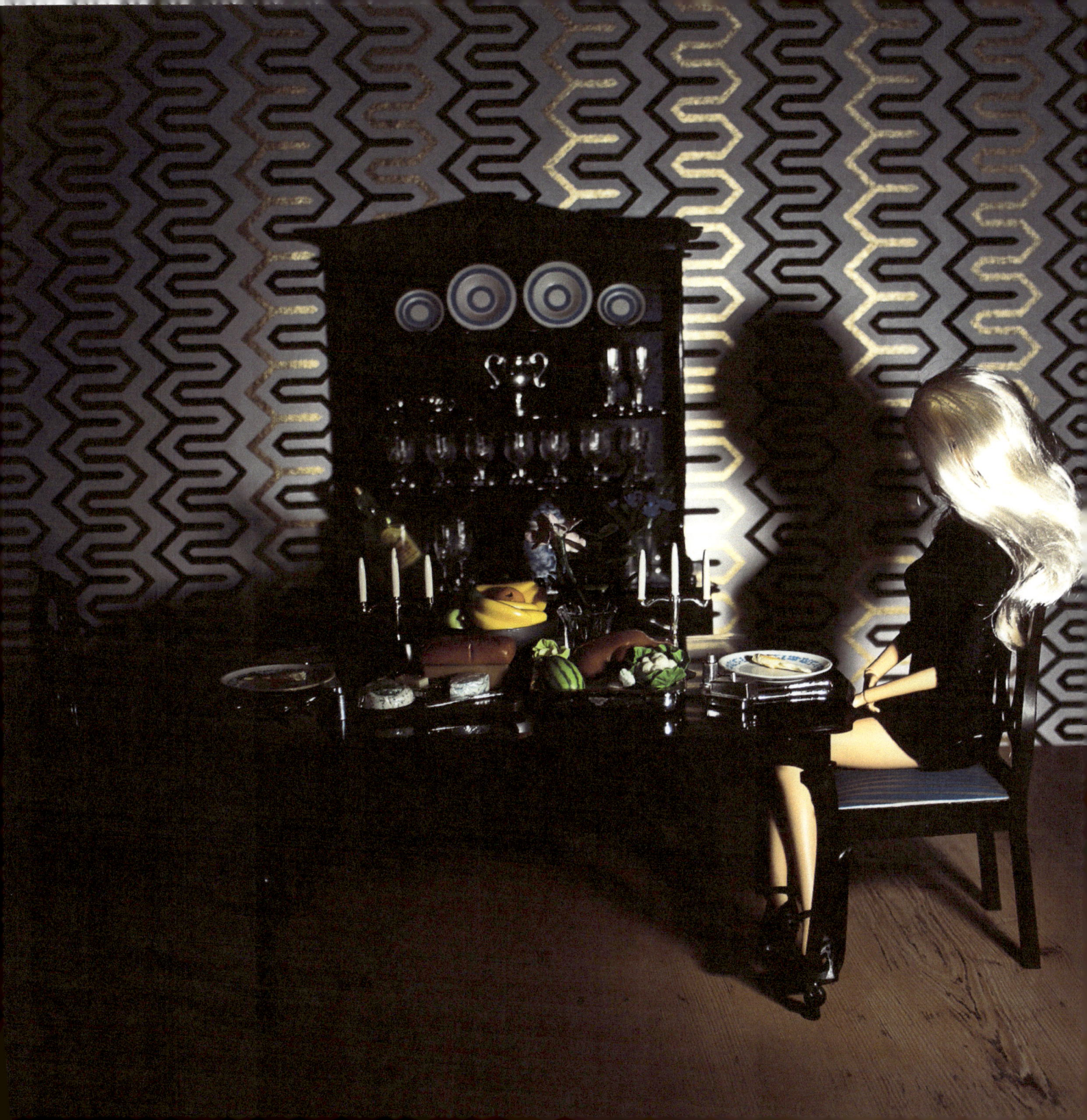

Now Barbie knew that ken was
a queer, she called her
friends to have a beer.

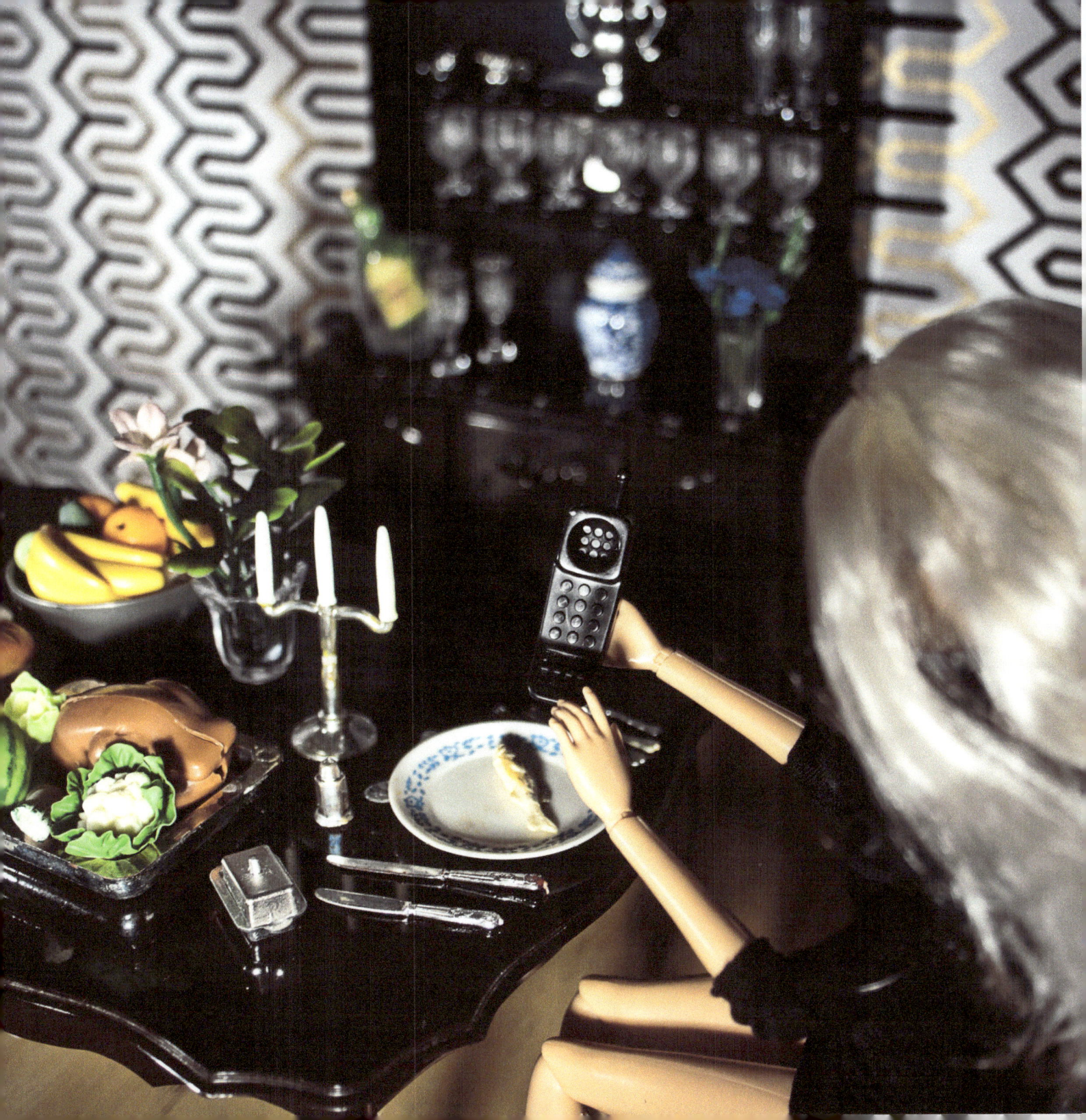

Barbie was livid, she felt like a sucker. Her friends chorused It s his fault, that fucker.

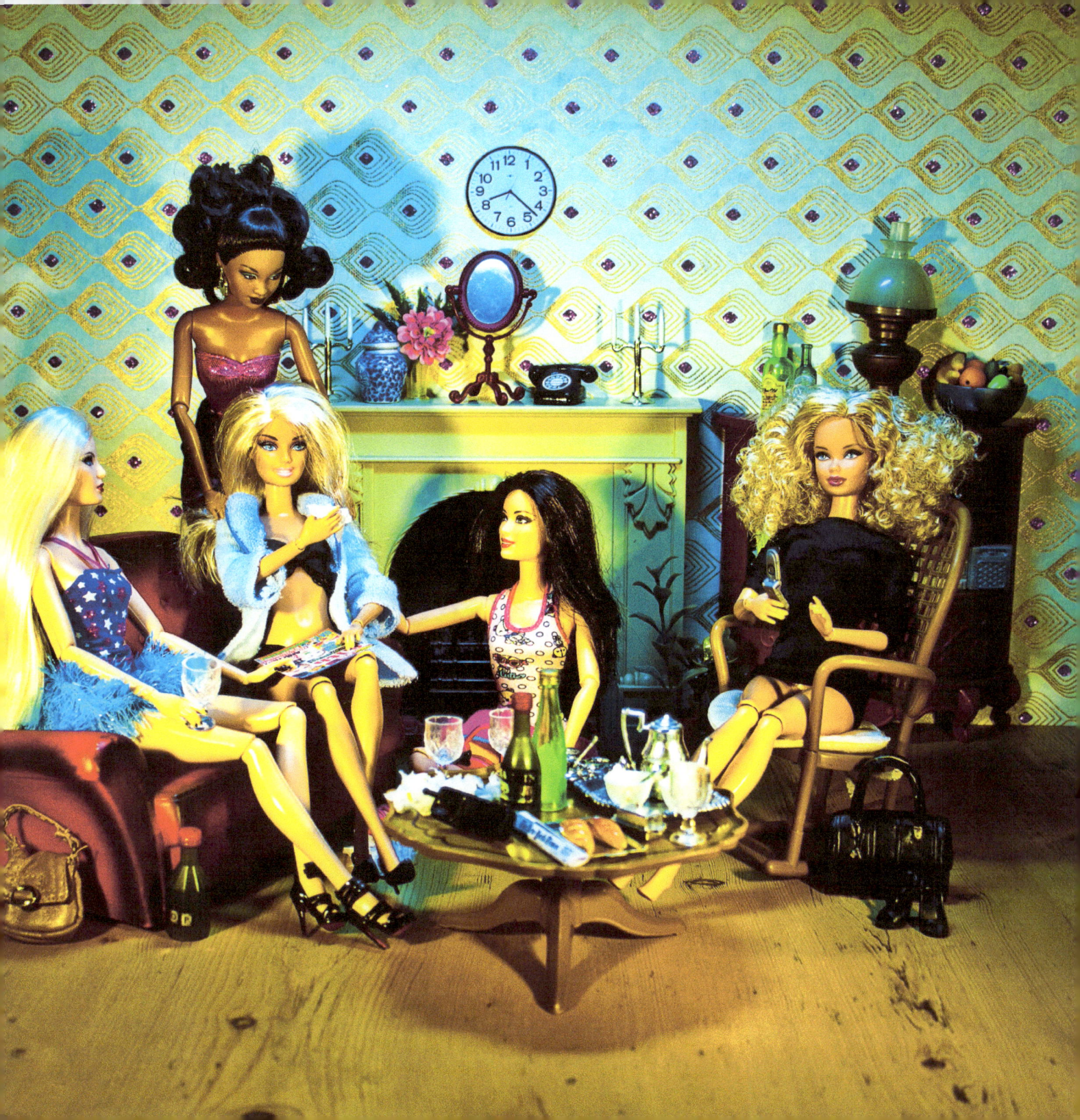

Ken stumbled in, late at night.
Barbie was waiting, they
started to fight.

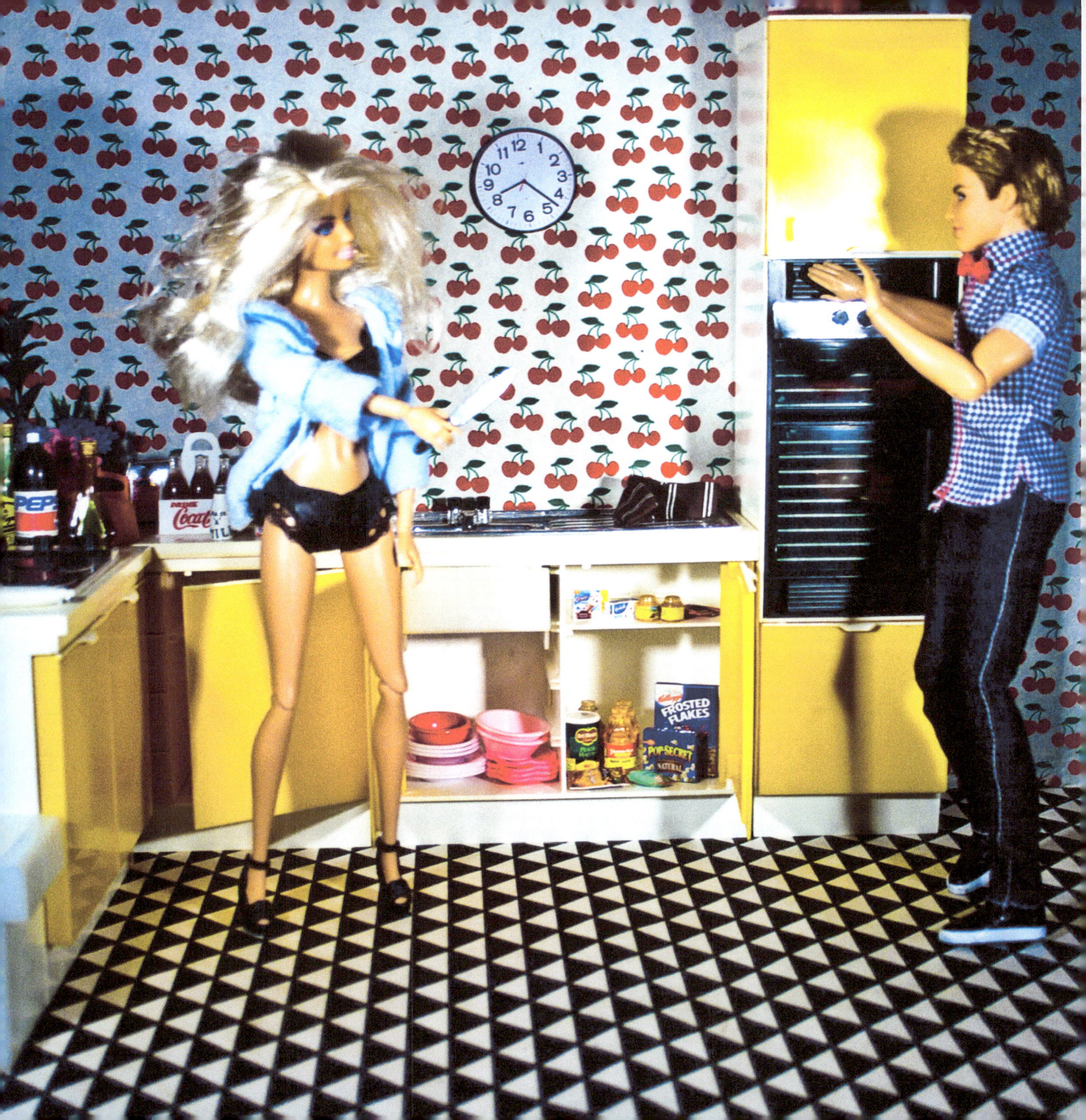

Barbie couldn t handle that
Ken liked men, he d lied and
he d cheated again and again.

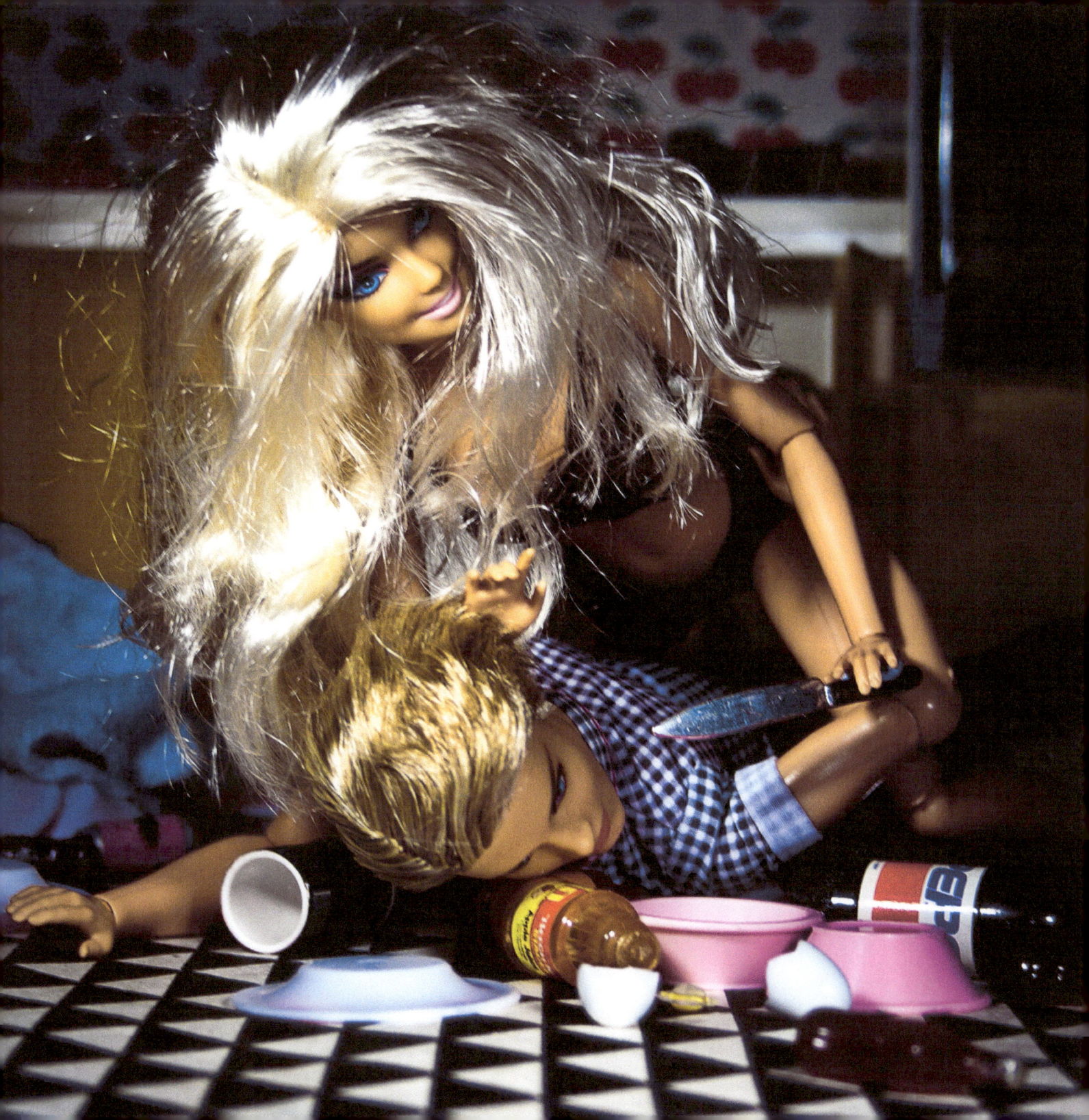

In the grips of despair, Barbie was lost. She wanted to end it, at any cost.

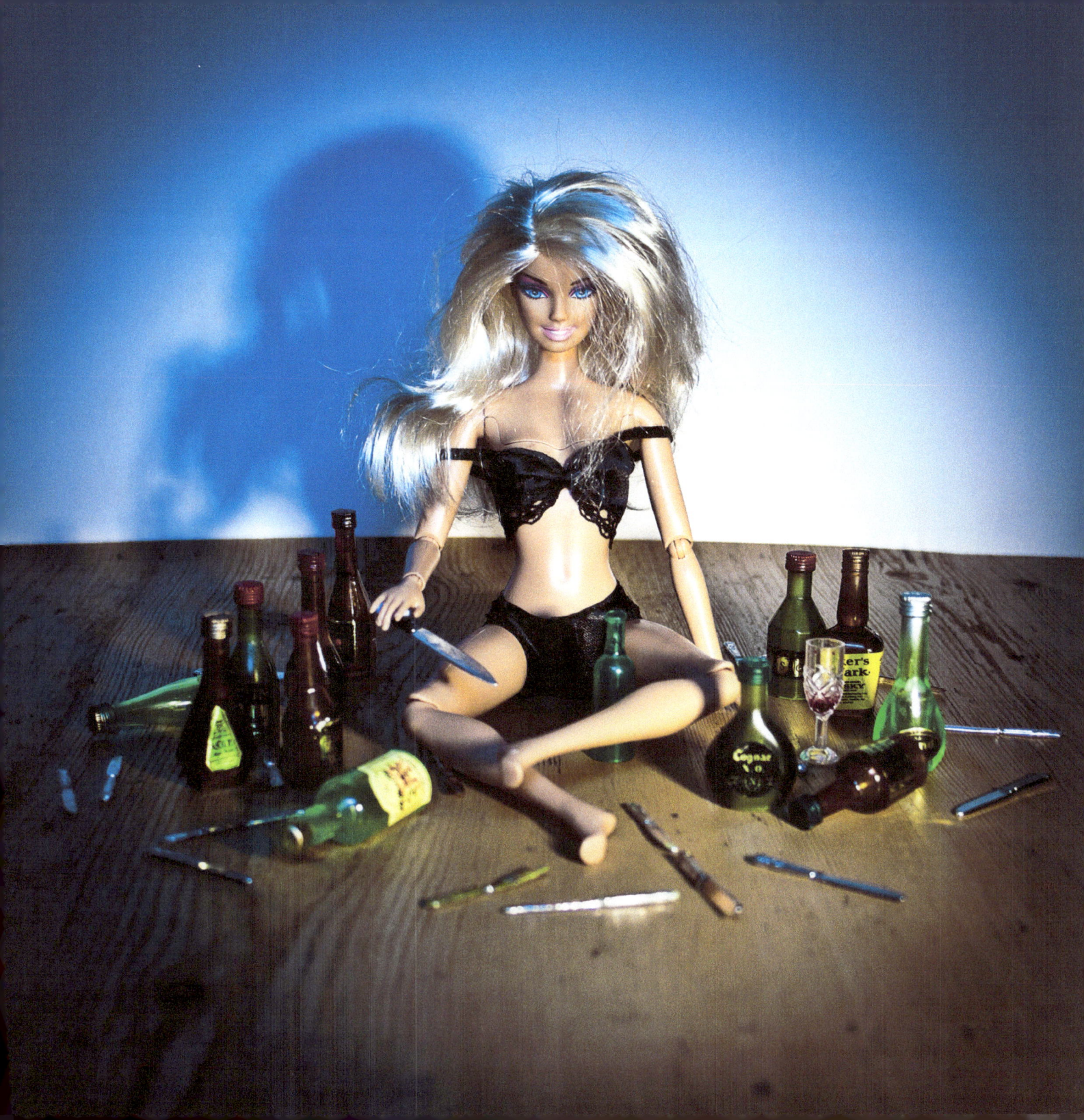

Into the bathroom, she tripped
and stumbled. Slitting her
wrists, her world had crumbled.

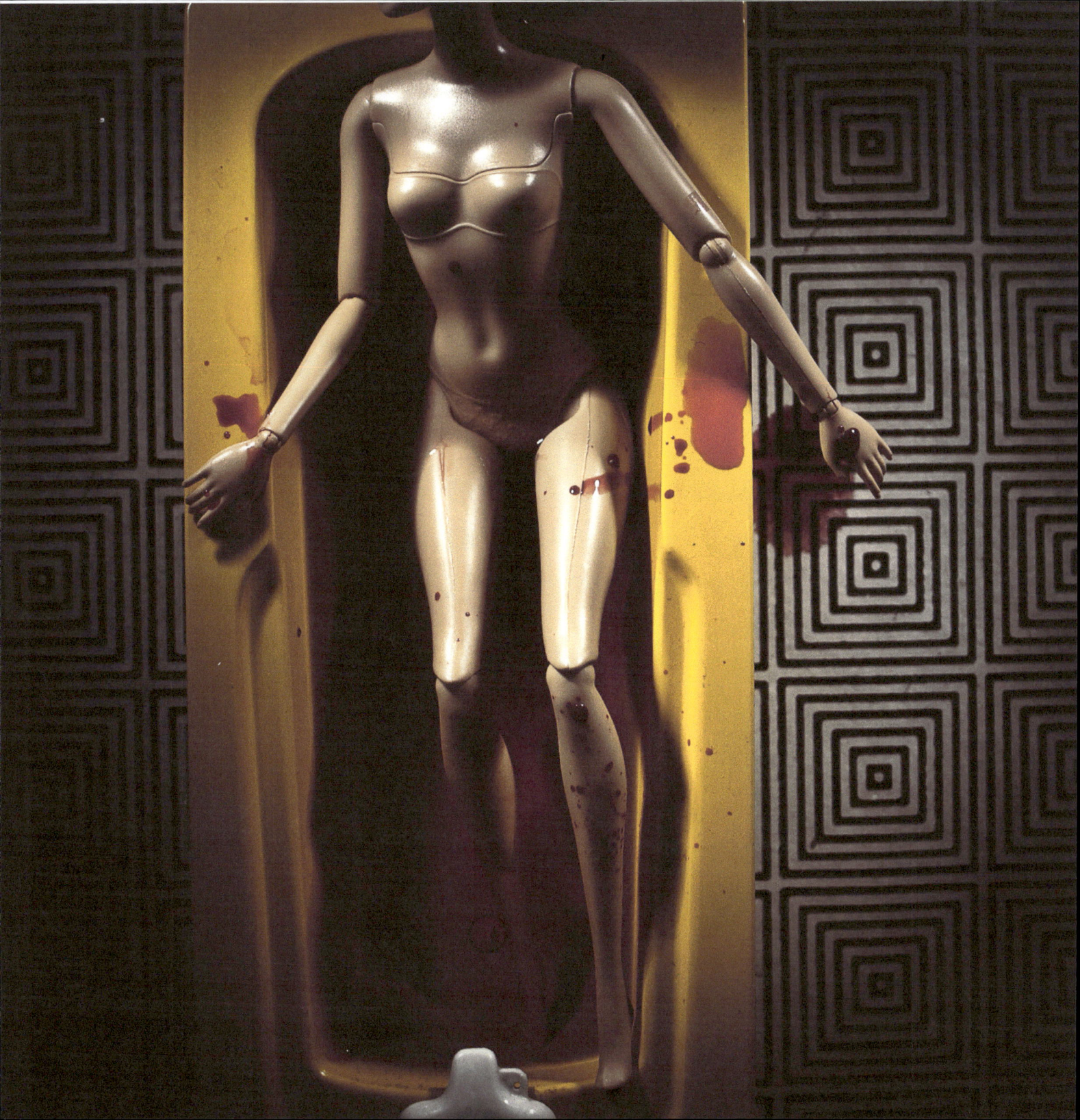

Upon hearing the news of Barbies attempt, Ken s resolve cracked. His fun was spent.

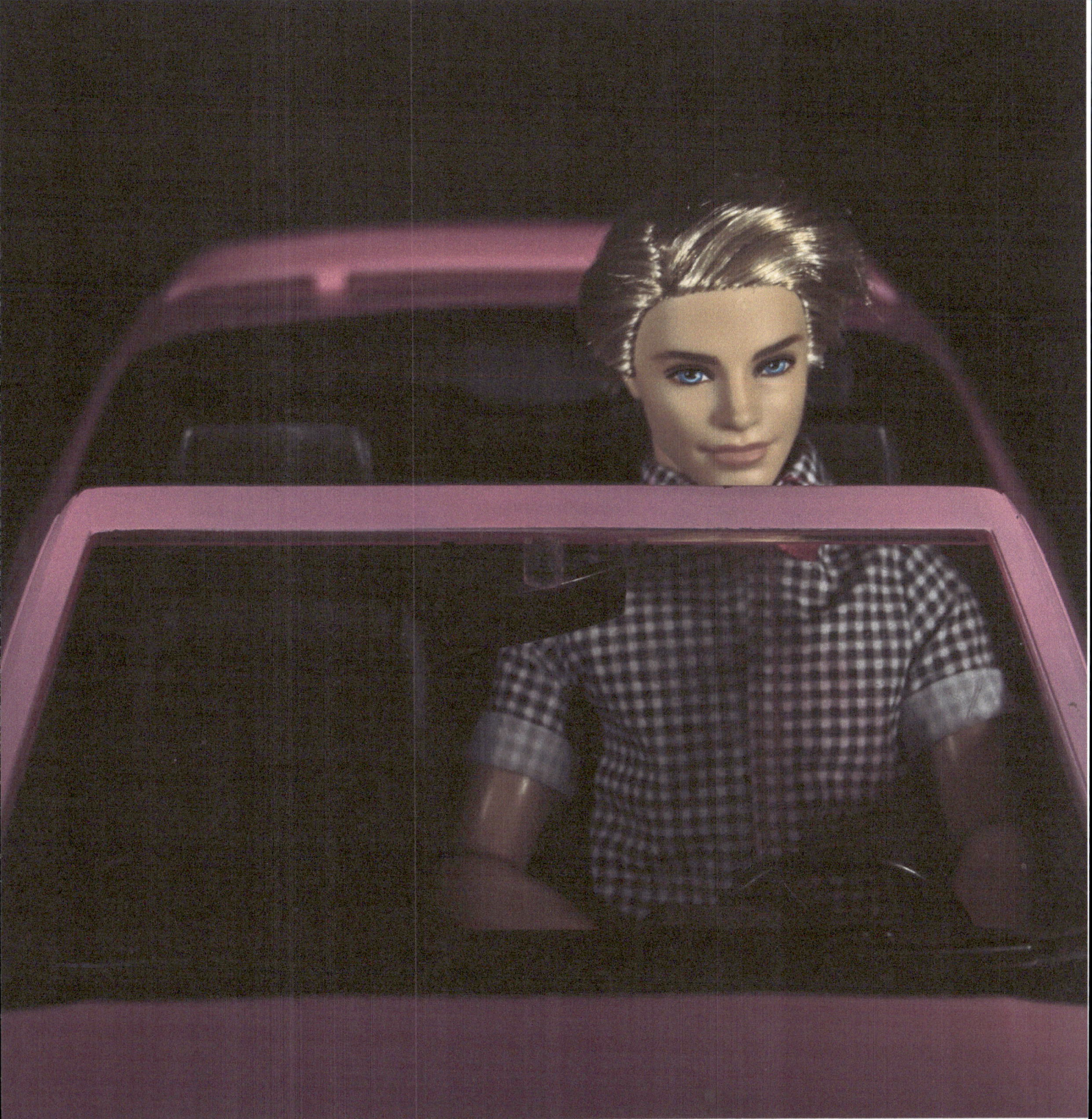

Full of guilt, Ken rushed to his bride. Despite his true feelings he d stay by her side.

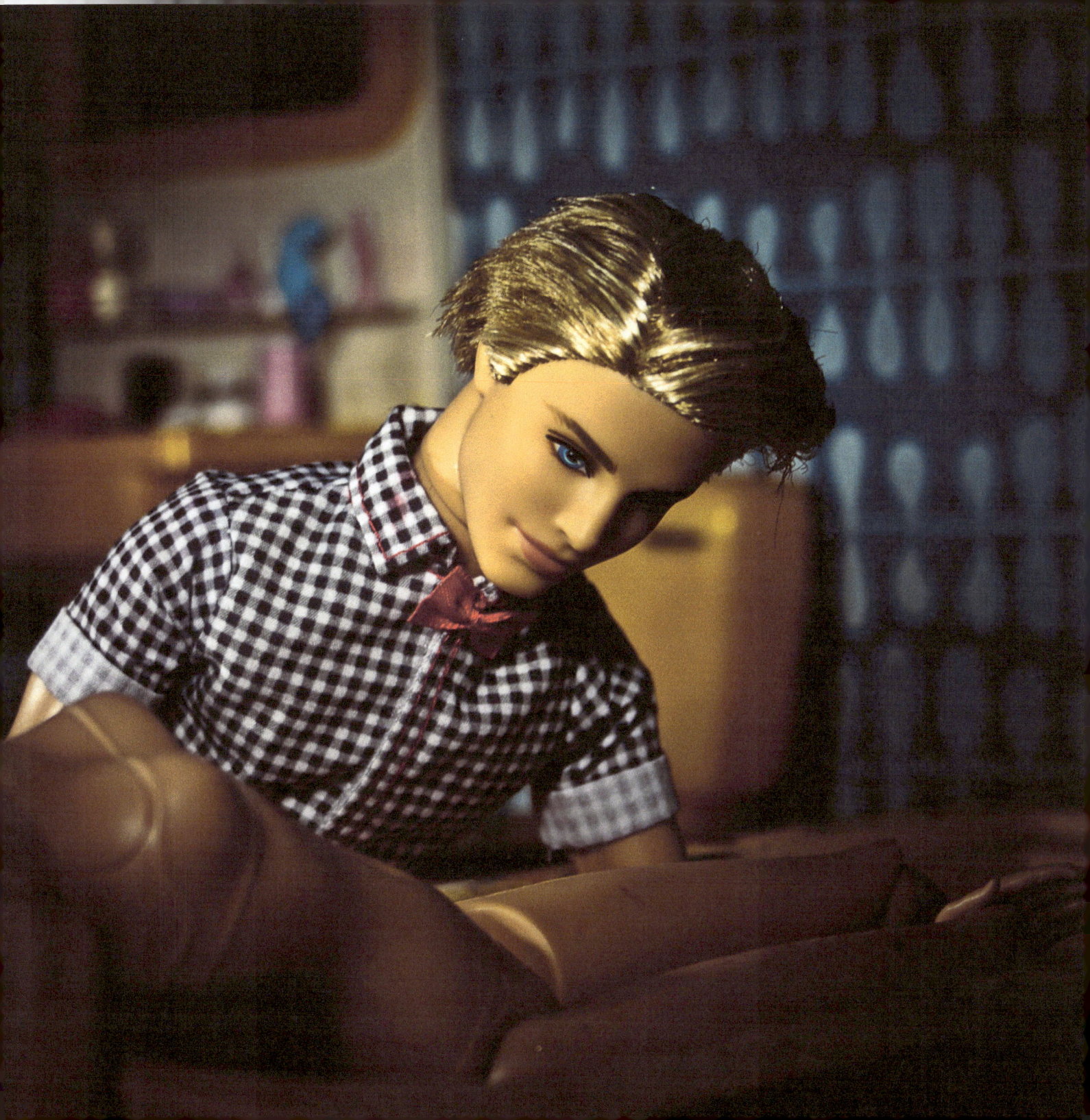

Barbie being Barbie accepted
his plea, and they lived
together not so happily.

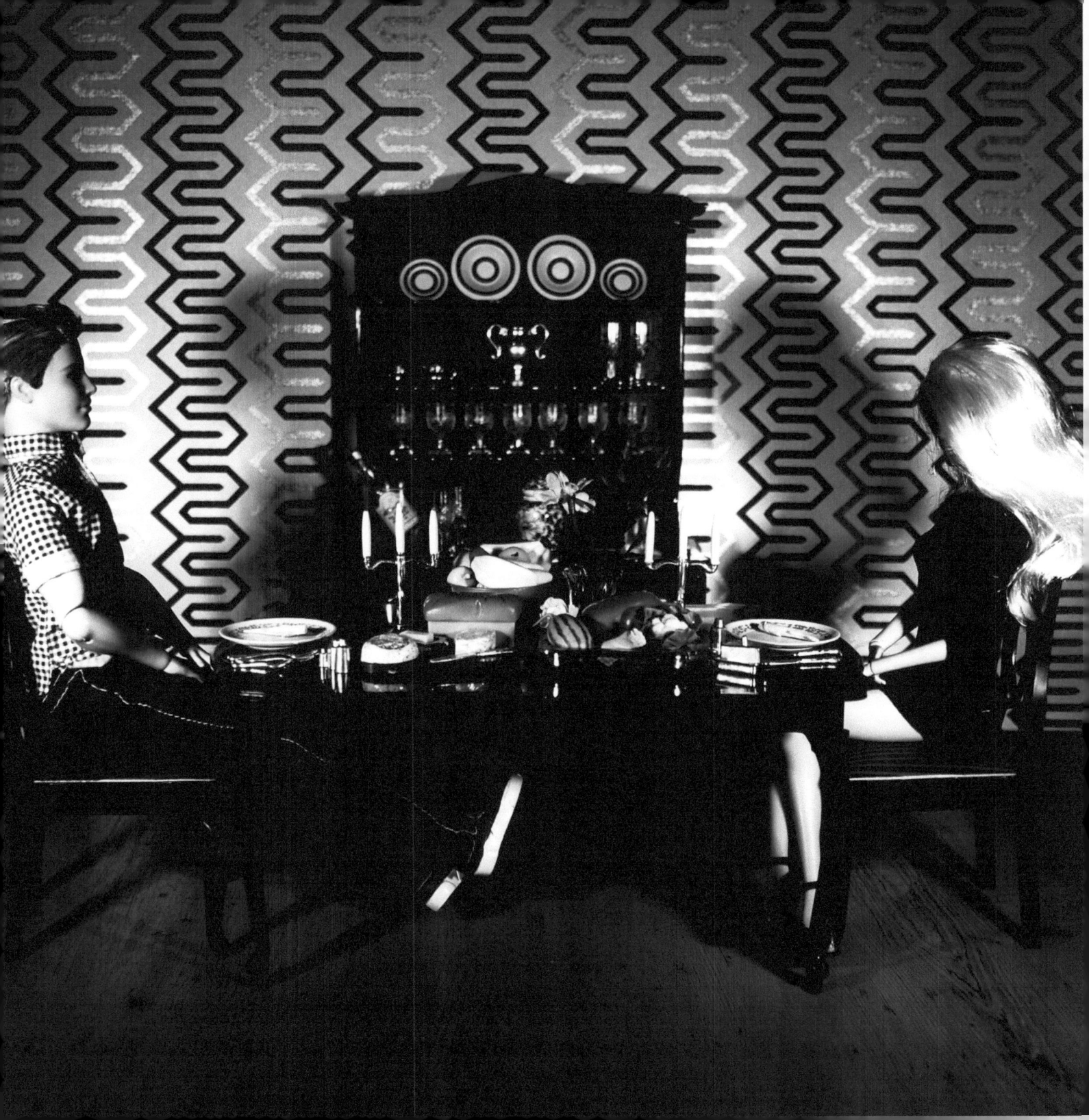

END

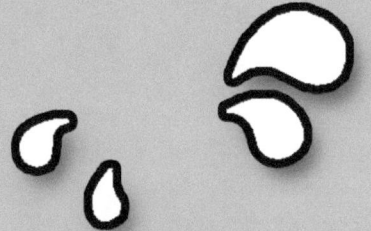

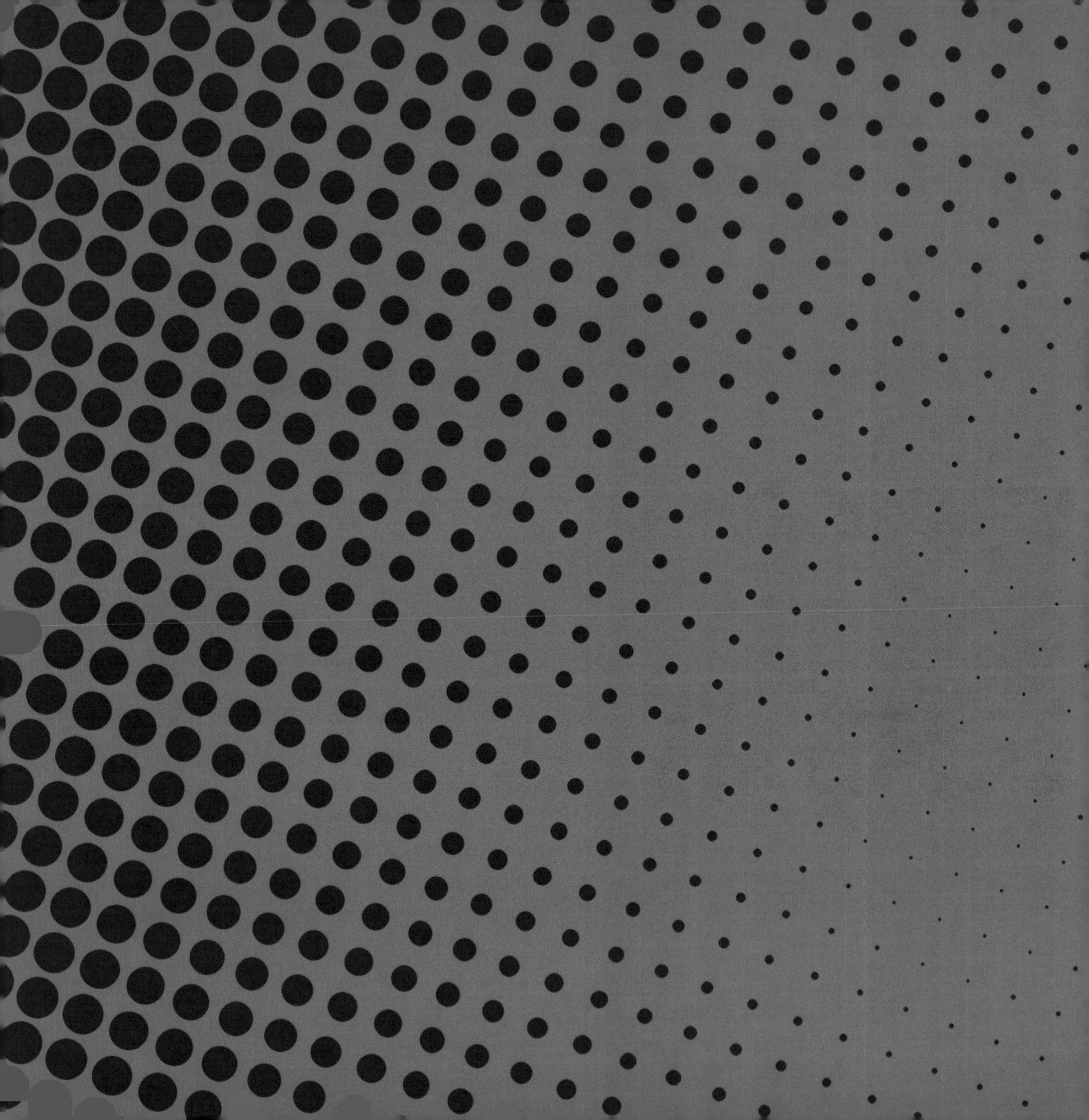

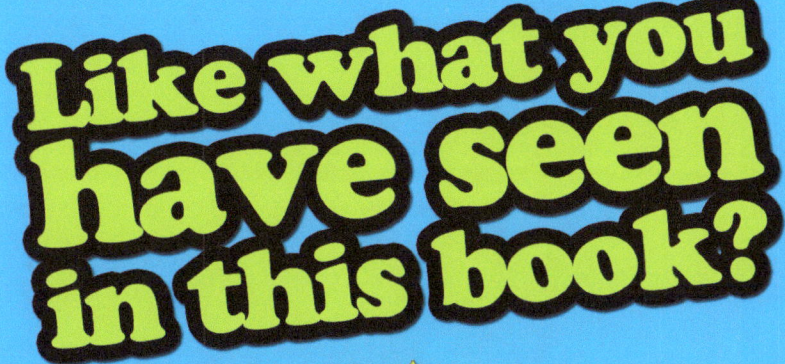

Like what you have seen in this book?

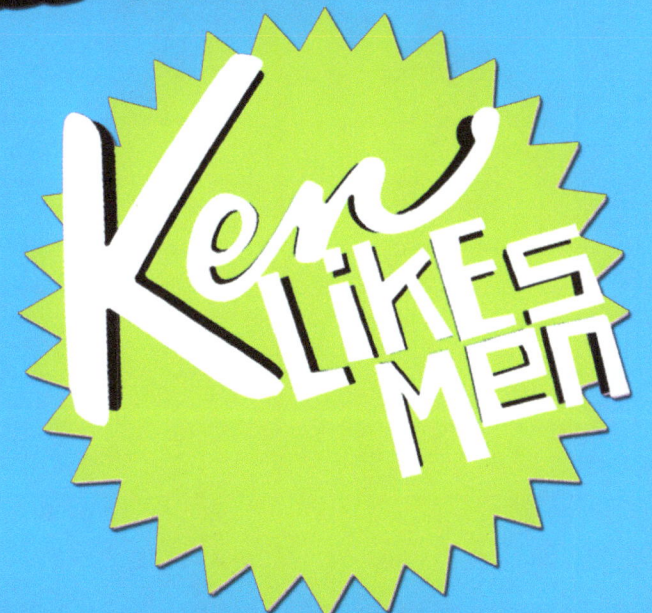

Ken LIKES men

Check out more at facebook

facebook.com/kenlikesmen

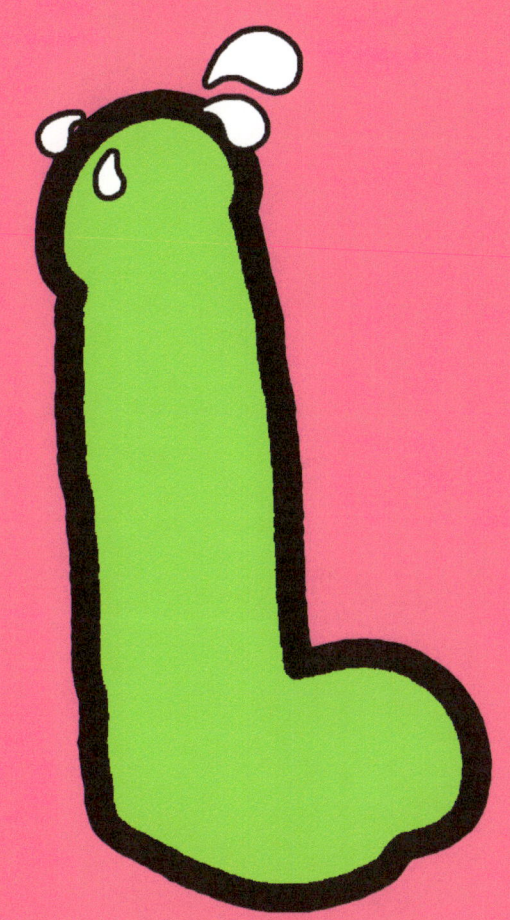

COMPETITION

Like us on: facefuck®

Tweet us on: twatter

for your chance to win a tanning set!

T&C: THIS IS ALL BULL SHIT.

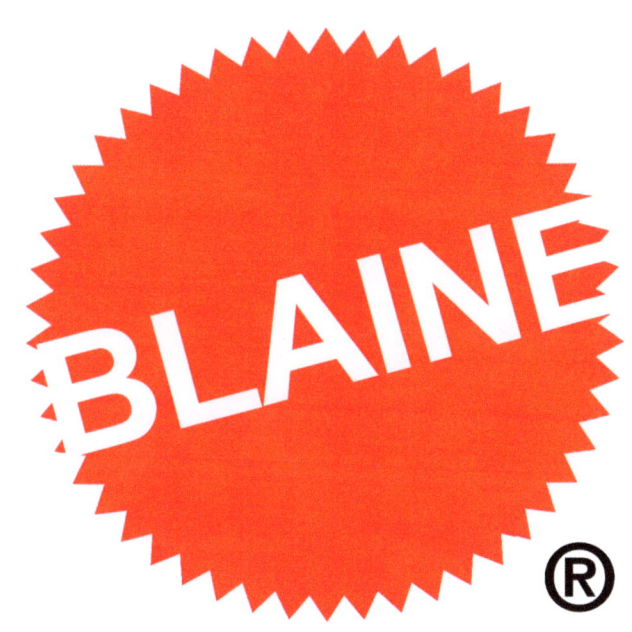

FREE COUPON

CUT THIS OUT, TAKE IT TO YOUR NEAREST STORE, AND EXPECT ABSOLUTELY SHIT ALL FOR FREE!

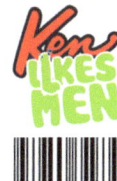

Honestly we are not kidding, this coupon gives you nothing! If you do not believe us please try it out for yourself. Ken Likes Men will not be hold responsible for anyone who makes a tit out of themselves and will not pay out anything for your discomfort and embarrassment. PS. You are an idiot, now you have ruined this book! For more fabulous freebies visit www.facebook.com/kenlikesmen *Giveaways* never.

www.ingramcontent.com/pod-product-compliance
Lightning Source LLC
Chambersburg PA
CBHW051050180526
45172CB00002B/577